First American Edition 2000 by Kane/Miller Book Publishers
La Jolla, California

Originally produced in Great Britain in 1998 by Andersen Press, Ltd. as a
special edition for Domestos Hygiene Advisory Service for promotional purposes only.

First American paperback, 2000

Library of Congress Cataloging-in-Publication Data

Ross, Tony
Wash your hands!/Tony Ross. – 1st American ed.
p. cm.
"A Cranky Nell Book"
Summary: When a little princess hears about germs and nasties living all around her,
she understands the importance of washing her hands a lot.

[1. Hand washing –Fiction. 2. Cleanliness – Fiction 3. Princesses – Fiction.] I. Title
PZ7.R71992 Was 2000   [E] – dc21   00-022090

ISBN 1-929132-01-8 (pbk)

Printed and bound in Singapore by Tien Wah Press Pte. Ltd.
3 4 5 6 7 8 9 10

Wash Your Hands!

Tony Ross

A CRANKY NELL BOOK

Kane/Miller
BOOK PUBLISHERS

"Wheeeeeeeeeee!"
The Little Princess LOVED getting dirty."

"Wash your hands before you eat that,"
said the Queen.
"Why?" said the Little Princess.

"Because you've been playing outside,"
said the Queen.

"Wash your hands," said the Cook.
"Why?" said the Little Princess.

"Because you've been playing with Scruff.
And dry them properly."

"Wash your hands," said the King.
"Why? I've washed them TWICE,"
said the Little Princess.

"And you must wash them again
because you've just been on your potty."

"Wash your hands," said the Maid.

"I washed them after playing outside.
I washed them after playing with the dog.
I washed them after going on my potty.
I washed them after sneezing . . ."

". . . WHY?" said the Little Princess.
"Because of germs and nasties," said the Maid.
"What are germs and nasties?" said the Little Princess.

"They're HORRIBLE!" said the Maid.

"They live in the dirties . . .

. . . and on the animals . . .

. . . and in the sneezes.

Then they can get into your food,
and then into your tummy . . .

. . . and then they make you ill."

"What do germs and nasties look like?" said the Little Princess.
"Worse than crocodiles," said the Maid.

"I've got no crocodiles on MY hands."

"Germs and nasties are smaller than crocodiles,"
said the Maid.
"They are too small to see."

"I'd better wash my hands again," said the Little Princess.

"Do I have to wash my hands after washing my hands?"

"Don't be silly," said the Maid.
"Eat your cake."

"Have you washed YOUR hands?"